Essential Events

The Louisiana Purchase

Essential Events

The Louisiana Purchase

by Jon Zurn

Content Consultant
G. Howard Hunter
Louisiana Historical Society

ABDO
Publishing Company

CREDITS

Published by ABDO Publishing Company, 8000 West 78th Street, Edina, Minnesota 55439. Copyright © 2008 by Abdo Consulting Group, Inc. International copyrights reserved in all countries. No part of this book may be reproduced in any form without written permission from the publisher. The Essential Library™ is a trademark and logo of ABDO Publishing Company.

Printed in the United States.

Editor: Paula Lewis
Cover Design: Becky Daum
Interior Design: Lindaanne Donohoe

Library of Congress Cataloging-in-Publication Data
Zurn, Jon.
   The Louisiana Purchase / Jon Zurn
      p. cm.—(Essential events)
   Includes bibliographical references and index.
   ISBN-13: 978-1-59928-853-6
   1. Louisiana Purchase—Juvenile literature. 2. United States—Territorial expansion—Juvenile literature. 3. Napoleon I, Emperor of the French, 1769-1821—Juvenile literature. I. Title.
E333.Z86 2008
973.4'6—dc22
                           2007012008

The Louisiana Purchase

TABLE OF CONTENTS

Chapter 1	A Surprise Meeting	6
Chapter 2	To the Frontier	14
Chapter 3	Louisiana: The New World Colony	24
Chapter 4	The Shifting Balance of Power	34
Chapter 5	Napoleon's Vision of Empire	46
Chapter 6	The American Dilemma: Jefferson Pursues Peace	54
Chapter 7	The Twists of Fate	64
Chapter 8	The Louisiana Purchase	74
Chapter 9	The Nation Doubles in Size Overnight	82
Chapter 10	The New America	90

Timeline	96
Essential Facts	100
Additional Resources	102
Glossary	104
Source Notes	106
Index	109
About the Author	112

Chapter 1

Robert Livingston

A Surprise Meeting

Robert Livingston, the U.S. minister to France, had suffered a frustrating day. Now he faced a man he knew well as a corrupt politician, a liar, and a cheat. Charles Maurice de Talleyrand, France's minister of foreign affairs,

The Louisiana Purchase

unexpectedly called Livingston to his office. The American had no idea what Talleyrand wanted, but Livingston had enough on his mind. The next day, April 12, 1803, James Monroe would arrive in Paris with secret instructions from President Thomas Jefferson. Livingston did not know Monroe's exact orders. However, he did know that Monroe was to negotiate a single serious issue with the French.

Livingston had worked hard to reach a deal with the French on the same issue. For 14 months, the diplomat had tried to negotiate with the French leader, Napoleon Bonaparte. Livingston plotted strategies, wrote letters and pamphlets, made friends with corrupt officials, offered threats and allegiances—all to convince Napoleon to agree to a land deal. The United States wanted to buy New Orleans, the valuable port along the Mississippi River.

America also was interested in the territories known as Eastern and Western Florida (modern-day Florida and southern portions of Alabama and Mississippi).

> **A Troubled Start**
>
> In 1803, the United States was an infant nation. The former 13 colonies had agreed to the U.S. Constitution just 15 years earlier. Rival leaders still argued bitterly over how to govern. Though it lost the Revolutionary War, England remained a constant threat. Many believed the United States would one day be a great nation, but first it had to get on its feet.

A Troubling Turn of Events

In 1801, the United States was still recovering from the Revolutionary War. The country was growing. Pioneers moved to new territory as far west as the Mississippi River. Settlers in territories such as Kentucky, Ohio, and Tennessee used the great river to carry their goods to the port city of New Orleans. There, river flatboats loaded with wheat, lumber, and furs met with buyers who sent the goods to cities along the Atlantic coast, England, France, and Spain. In 1801, the "West"—an area between the Appalachian Mountains and the Mississippi River—was mostly unsettled and wild. America's leaders understood that the resources of the West and the port of New Orleans were vital to prosperity.

However, Spain ruled the port city of New Orleans. Spain controlled Mexico, much of South America, several Caribbean islands, as well as Eastern and Western Florida. Spain also controlled the Louisiana territory which included all the land west of the Mississippi River and north to the border with British-controlled Canada. The territory was mostly uncharted wilderness. For Spain, only New Orleans was important. Whoever controlled New Orleans could charge port fees and taxes for goods delivered and

The Louisiana Purchase

shipped from there and on goods carried along the Mississippi River.

The United States was on good terms with Spain. The Spanish agreed to allow free passage for American ships and tax-free storage of American goods at New Orleans. Without the high costs of shipping and taxes, U.S. profits increased.

Ugly Rumors

In 1801, rumors circulated that Spain no longer ruled New Orleans. Reports came of a secret treaty between King Charles IV of Spain and Napoleon Bonaparte of France. The agreement had supposedly turned over Eastern and Western Florida and all of Louisiana, including New Orleans, to the French. If that were true, France would have a major colony in North America. Napoleon had ambitions to acquire new territory. Louisiana was an incredible opportunity.

Speculation rose to fear. If France took control of Louisiana, hopes for U.S. western expansion would be cut off at the Mississippi. The port of New Orleans might close to free trade. Napoleon could have ideas about pushing eastward.

Many Americans wanted war. Some threatened to raise armies and march on New Orleans before the

French arrived. But President Jefferson demanded restraint. He was alarmed by the rumors, but he knew his country was not ready for another war. The better option was a peaceful settlement. However, he would have to act quickly.

Livingston's Troubles in France

These were the issues that led President Jefferson to select Livingston to negotiate with France. A talented debater and shrewd negotiator, Livingston had served in the Continental Congress and

---

New Orleans

New Orleans was a major port city by the time Napoleon laid claim to it. Situated at the mouth of the Mississippi River, where the waterway meets the Gulf of Mexico, the city made a perfect port for trade.

The French explorer and soldier Jean Baptist Le Moyne de Bienville founded the city in 1718. He chose the land for its natural protection from Gulf storms and enemy warships. At first, New Orleans was laid out as a military outpost, designed as a defense against local Native American tribes or British troops. Soon, though, a city emerged. French soldiers brought their wives and children. Other French settlers arrived, too. Businesses and culture grew. The city built schools, a theater, and the beautiful Cathedral of Saint Louis. Even after New Orleans was turned over to the Spanish in 1763, it kept its French roots.

With western expansion, Americans shipped goods down the Mississippi from as far north as present-day Minnesota. They sent fur, grains, lumber, cheese, dried meats, and other valuable products for sale in the South. New Orleans boomed as a center of shipping and trade.

French, American, German, Spanish, and other immigrants flocked to the city. Black slaves came from the Caribbean, bringing their own heritage. Together, all these diverse cultural groups blended into a unique society, rich with the flavors of many nations.

The Louisiana Purchase

helped draft the Declaration of Independence. On October 15, 1801, he sailed for Paris, France, to negotiate with Napoleon.

Upon his arrival and every day after, Livingston faced rejection. Napoleon refused to listen. Talleyrand denied that France had made a deal with Spain. Napoleon's brother, Joseph Bonaparte, also rejected Livingston's appeals. Every effort hit a dead end.

> **Emperor Forever**
>
> In 1800, Napoleon Bonaparte reigned like a dictator as sole ruler of France. By 1804, he named himself Emperor of France, a title he intended to keep for life.

Rumors grew stronger and more distressing. Livingston's informants reported that Napoleon planned to send 5,000 to 7,000 troops to its colony in the Caribbean, San Domingue (present-day Haiti). From there, the troops would go to New Orleans and take control of Louisiana. As the rumors spread, evidence of the treaty between France and Spain surfaced. The secret agreement was real. President Jefferson received a copy in May 1802.

The situation was desperate. What would happen if the French took New Orleans? What did Napoleon really want? Would there be war? Would the United States have to form an alliance with its old enemy, England, to fend off a French invasion? Secretary of

State James Madison wrote to Livingston, telling him to urge the French leader to sell New Orleans and the Floridas to the United States. President Jefferson would even accept French control of Louisiana. He did not want to go to war. But New Orleans was key. The United States had to have control of the port city.

Livingston argued with Bonaparte, hinted of war, yet offered peace and a simple solution: name the price. How much for New Orleans? Napoleon would hear none of it.

Success at Last

More than a year had gone by, and Livingston was no closer to a settlement. Napoleon had his treaty with Spain. He had ships, troops, and weapons ready for Louisiana. War seemed inevitable. Monroe was about to arrive in Paris, probably to take over where Livingston had failed.

The ornate office of the French foreign minister did little to brighten Livingston's spirits. Talleyrand was pleasant—a far cry from his usual arrogance. At last, the French foreign minister leaned forward and calmly asked if the United States would be interested in buying the entire Louisiana territory.

The Louisiana Purchase

Map of North America, circa 1798

Chapter 2

Announcement of the Treaty of Paris, 1783

To the Frontier

The Treaty of Paris in 1783 officially ended the American Revolution and acknowledged the new nation. After 15 years of rebellion and war, the old colonial empires of England, Spain, and France were forced to recognize a new nation.

The Louisiana Purchase

The new United States of America had successfully raised an army and driven the most powerful nation on Earth from prized North American land. It formed a government, coined its own money, and began trading with its neighbors.

The Treaty of Paris also meant the map of the New World had to be redrawn.

A Growing Country Looks Westward

For England, defeat meant retreat. Forced from its original 13 colonies, England gave up a source of wealth and a major foothold in the New World. It now had to settle for land to the north, in Canada, which was hardly as rich and developed as England's old Atlantic colonies.

The Treaty of Paris also granted Eastern and Western Florida, territory which had been held by England, to Spain. Spain's holdings now stretched from the Atlantic coast (present-day Florida) westward to include what is known today as the southern portions of Alabama, Mississippi, Louisiana, and Texas. The territory connected to Spain's rich colony, Mexico.

Before the U.S. Constitution

Before the Constitution was ratified, the 13 states were known as the Confederation of States. The United States considered itself a single nation under the Articles of Confederation, adopted in 1781, but it took six more years to agree on the Constitution.

France was not included in the 1783 treaty. Years before, it had controlled wide tracts of land west and north of England's American colonies. However, it lost its claims in wars against the British. Instead, the French kept their colony of San Domingue. This established and profitable island provided France with immense wealth and a place of influence in the New World.

The treaty also forced England to turn over control of land west of the 13 colonies to the new American nation. This included the Appalachian

> ### Navigating the Mississippi River
>
> Early farmers and traders navigated the Mississippi long before the American Revolution. They traveled down the many rivers leading to the Mississippi, then on to New Orleans to sell their goods. They constructed simple wooden rafts, flat beds of wooden planks held together with rope. They lashed down their bags and barrels and rode the river's current southward. A simple board served as a rudder to steer them clear of rapids and sandbars. Some learned to build pirogues, simple hollowed-out trees shaped like a canoe with a flat bottom, from the Indians.
>
> By the mid-1700s, flatboats became larger and more elaborate. They were still flat-bottomed but often supported a long structure with a roof, like a houseboat. The roof protected valuable cargo from bad weather. Without power of their own, the flatboats could take months to drift downstream. Once they arrived at port, the flatboats were usually taken apart, and their lumber was sold off. Traders had to return home on foot or horseback.
>
> Flatboats were later replaced by keelboats, which had oars and sails to help speed the trip. Keelboats could also return upstream against the current. By the time of the Louisiana Purchase, the keelboat had turned the Mississippi into a thriving highway, with merchants selling their goods up and down the river wherever new towns sprang up.

The Louisiana Purchase

Mountains and the wilderness that stretched all the way west to the Mississippi River. The territory was a vast expanse, extending from Canada south to Spain's holdings along the Gulf of Mexico. To the rebellious colonists, it was incredible enough that they had won control of their homeland along the Atlantic. Now they suddenly owned a huge territory to the west as well.

After the First Thirteen

The original 13 colonies became the first states of the newly formed United States. By 1803, Vermont, Kentucky, Tennessee, and Ohio had also become states.

Conquering the Frontier

Even before the American Revolution began in 1775, explorers and settlers had ventured over the Appalachians into the lush land beyond. To the south, in areas that later became Kentucky and Tennessee, farmers found fertile soil for their crops. In the Northwest Territory (what would later become Ohio, Indiana, Michigan, and Illinois), dense forests provided timber and wildlife for hunting and trapping. Little was known about the wild land. It seemed almost endless and filled with potential riches.

Slowly, settlers trickled westward, hoping to prosper. Eventually, trading posts and towns emerged. British troops mapped the territory and navigated the many rivers leading west. They built forts, even as far west as the Mississippi River, protecting their claims on the east bank, while the Spanish faced them from the west.

When the American Revolution ended, a pioneering boom quickly followed. Thousands of settlers, farmers, trappers, missionaries, and merchants poured from the east over the Appalachians. More towns grew up. The rivers served as flatboat highways for merchants. They carried everything from grain, pork, and fur to guns, pots, and pans. Flatboats traveled all the way from the Atlantic to the Spanish port city of New Orleans, where the Mississippi meets the Gulf of Mexico.

Though rugged and still a dangerous place, the western lands proved rich and profitable. By 1790, more than 120,000 people lived between the Appalachians and the Mississippi River.

Building the Nation

Four years passed after the Treaty of Paris before the 13 states unified as one nation. Leaders such as George Washington, Alexander Hamilton, Thomas Jefferson, and James Madison struggled to bring each independent state to agreement over a united single government. During those years, the 13 states held

The Louisiana Purchase

George Washington at the Constitutional Convention, 1787

together while representatives from each state worked out rules, regulations, and laws for a central, federal government. Finally, in 1787, they reached an agreement, and the first seven articles of the Constitution were adopted. The nation could truly call itself the United States of America.

Settlers moving west after the Revolutionary War

Through the process of building a government, leaders made clear plans for western expansion. By 1787, much of the western frontier fell under the ownership of the new federal government.

The Northwest Ordinance of 1787 established plans for governing the region west of Pennsylvania and

The Louisiana Purchase

north of the Ohio River. It set up rules for councils, courts, and militias. When an area included at least 5,000 free male citizens of voting age, it could send a non-voting delegate to Congress. Once an area within the territory achieved 60,000 residents, it could join the nation as a fellow state. The rules under the Northwest Ordinance paved the way for future territories to one day become states of the Union. In 1792, Kentucky became the first state west of the Appalachians. Tennessee followed in 1796. Both states made their western borders on the banks of the Mississippi River.

Leadership Looks West

Many American leaders recognized the incredible potential of the West, with its wide-open spaces and abundant natural resources. A small nation could grow larger and more powerful by expanding westward.

President George Washington encouraged western settlement under strong federal leadership. In 1794, he faced the first challenge to central-government rule. When the federal government imposed a tax on whiskey, settlers in Pennsylvania angrily rose up in armed protest, threatening to rebel. Washington called a militia of 13,000 troops that put down the "Whiskey

Rebellion" within days. This set the standard for establishing national-government rule over far-reaching western settlements.

Thomas Jefferson, the U.S. minister to France, was also a firm supporter of western expansion. He saw his nation rising in strength as it grew westward. He encouraged settlement, even into Spanish-held territory, believing the presence of U.S. settlers would one day bring the region into American hands. He envisioned the day when his nation stretched all the way to the Pacific Ocean. In a letter to James Monroe, Jefferson wrote:

> *However our present interests may restrain us within our own limits, it is impossible not to look forward to distant times, when our rapid multiplication will expand itself beyond those limits and cover the whole northern, if not the southern continent, with a people speaking the same language, governed in similar forms, and by similar laws.*[1]

When Jefferson became the third president of the United States in 1801, he believed his country was well on its way to expanding its borders.

The Louisiana Purchase

Thomas Jefferson

Chapter 3

Louisiana in the 1800s

Louisiana: The New World Colony

President Jefferson believed the future of his nation lay in the West. It was a future built on the hard-won successes of the men and women on the frontier. The settlers of Tennessee, Kentucky, and the Northwest Territory were slowly turning the

The Louisiana Purchase

wilderness into a thriving network of farms, towns, ports, and river highways. Flatboats on the Mississippi River carried goods to New Orleans. Jefferson calculated that approximately one-third of the nation's wealth came from the frontier.

Beyond the Mississippi

It was natural to look even further west, beyond the Mississippi River, though no one knew just how large the area was or what riches it had to offer. The Spanish, who governed Louisiana Territory in 1800, knew little of the area. In the prior 200 years, few explorers had ventured into its wilderness, and no one had reported anything of remarkable value.

Still, Jefferson believed that one day Louisiana could prove important to his nation's ambitions. He was not the first to believe this.

Louisiana, the French Colony

Not long after Columbus arrived in the New World, Spanish conquistadors pushed far westward,

Native American Lands

Thousands of Native Americans lived along the Mississippi River at the time of European exploration. Tribes included the Ojibwa, Winnebago, Fox, Choctaw, Sauk, Natchez, Alabama, and Chickasaw. The French and Spanish fought often with the tribes for control of land but sometimes made treaties to secure peace. Already, the British had pushed countless Native Americans westward. Strife between the Europeans and natives would only worsen.

into the Gulf of Mexico. In the search for passage to the Pacific Ocean, Alonzo Álvarez Pineda discovered the mouth of the Mississippi River in 1519. Others followed, but it was not for another 160 years that a nation would assert a serious claim on the region.

On April 9, 1682, a group of French explorers completed a three-month journey down the Mississippi River. They came from Fort Crevecoeur (Broken Heart) near present-day Peoria, Illinois, to the banks at the river's mouth where it fanned into a wide delta, emptying into the Gulf of Mexico. A large cross on a post painted with the French coat of arms was planted on the riverbank. Their leader, René Robert Cavelier Sieur de La Salle, announced:

> I ... do now take in the name of his Majesty, and of his successors to the Crown, possess of this country of Louisiana, the seas, harbors, ports, bays, adjacent straits, and all the nations, peoples, provinces, cities, towns, villages, mines, minerals, fisheries, streams, and rivers within the extent of said Louisiana ... .[1]

La Salle declared the land they had just traveled and the territory east and west—wherever rivers flowed to the great Mississippi—now belonged to King Louis XIV of France. La Salle named the expanse Louisiana.

The Louisiana Purchase

La Salle claimed the expanse of land he had explored for France and named it Louisiana.

Having only explored a small sliver of the land he claimed, La Salle could not have known how vast Louisiana really was. The territory covered the area between the Rocky Mountains and the Appalachian Mountains, with the Mississippi River running down the center. Unexplored wilderness stretched between the mountain ranges.

Essential Events

For France, the claim was important. La Salle had extended French power deep into the heart of the New World. His declaration laid claim to a major piece of the continent. Louisiana sat like a giant wedge between Spanish claims along the Pacific and British colonies on the Atlantic.

By 1699, the first French settlers arrived on the Mississippi. In 1718, the port village of New Orleans was founded and quickly became a thriving center of trade.

As France continued its quest to colonize the New World, England reacted with its own plans. The

---

Explorers on the Mississippi

Hernando de Soto was probably the first European explorer to venture far inland to the Mississippi River, which he called the *Rio de Espiritu Santo* (River of the Holy Spirit). In 1540–1541, he crossed the southeastern territories (Georgia, the Carolinas, Tennessee, and Alabama) and explored along the Mississippi River. Fighting with Indians, starvation, and de Soto's death a year later deemed the effort a disaster. About the same time, Francisco de Coronado ventured inland from the west. He led an expedition out of Mexico and across present-day Arizona and New Mexico in search of fabled cities of gold. His expedition traveled eastward into the area now known as Kansas. Finding no riches, de Coronado returned to Mexico.

French explorers ventured from the north more than 100 years later, coming through the Great Lakes and across present-day Wisconsin. Father Jacques Marquette, a missionary, and the explorer Louis Jolliet took canoes down the Mississippi in 1673. They traveled down river to less than 450 miles (725 km) from its mouth. As they neared the mouth of the Arkansas River, they met Indians carrying European goods. Fearing they may encounter the Spanish, they turned back. In 1682, Sieur de La Salle claimed the region.

The Louisiana Purchase

ambitious nations came into constant conflict. In 1754, a decisive war broke out between France and England. Each country allied with different warring Native American tribes. Known as the French and Indian War, the struggle continued for nine years.

> **A Leader**
> One of the first battles of the French and Indian War was led by a 21-year-old lieutenant colonel named George Washington. He later drove the British from its colonies and became the first president of the United States of America.

When England finally defeated France in 1763, it forced its rival to relinquish half of Louisiana, from the Mississippi eastward. France also had to give up its holdings in Canada. As punishment for supporting France, Spain was forced to give up control of East and West Florida, which stretched from present-day Louisiana to Georgia. The British now controlled virtually all the land east of the Mississippi between Canada and the Gulf of Mexico.

The Spanish Colony

After 100 years of colonial ambition, losing the French and Indian War was a crushing blow for France. What remained of their holdings in North America was a distant wilderness even the British did not want. French King Louis XV turned his focus on his

Caribbean colonies. San Domingue, Martinique, and Guadeloupe provided a bounty of resources, especially sugar, providing a steady stream of wealth.

After the British carved out their eastern portion, Louis XV gave the rest of Louisiana to his cousin, King Charles III of Spain. He secretly offered it as a reward for Spain's help in the failed war and in compensation for their loss of the Floridas. Perhaps this would rebuild an alliance between the two nations in case England pursued further war.

At the time, Spain was a weakened nation, barely equal to its European rivals. Its holdings in the New World were still immense, but France and England had slowly made their own strongholds. Now, with the French driven out, England seemed poised for more colonial conquests. British troops had built a fort on the east bank of the Mississippi only 80 miles (129 km) north of New Orleans. What if they pushed westward? That would put a powerful enemy at the doorstep of one of Spain's most valuable possessions, the colony of Mexico. Fear of England forced Charles III to accept Louis XV's offer of Louisiana.

The king of Spain saw little future for Louisiana. Only the port at New Orleans offered any promise of profit. With the growth of settlements along the

The Louisiana Purchase

Mississippi, more and more goods passed through the port city. That meant taxes for the crown, a sum that grew greater every year. The rest of Louisiana, however, would have to wait to turn a profit. Spain's interests in Mexico, the Caribbean, and South America were more pressing.

> **Not Enough Gold**
>
> Spain was not as interested in colonization as the British and French were. The Spanish wanted the land for its potential gold and silver, which they had found in Mexico and South America. As it turned out, Louisiana had few riches of that kind.

For France, King Louis XV's gift meant that the once-mighty colonial power would no longer have a presence in North America. To many French people, it was a shameful loss. Some vowed that one day Louisiana would return to their hands.

This secret exchange between France and Spain in 1762 was barely noticed in the New World. French settlers in Louisiana did not learn of the treaty until two years after the agreement, and no Spanish officials arrived to govern for an additional two years. Even then, the culture and customs of the region were so solidly French that the change in power had little impact on the local way of life. The Spanish found themselves unpopular masters of an unruly society. The first Spanish governor, Don Antonio de Ulloa, fled from office after the residents of New Orleans threatened his life. General Alexander O'Reilly, the second governor, took the opposite approach, trying to crush any opposition. But "Bloody" O'Reilly finally left as well, having failed to turn his citizens into Spaniards.

The third governor, Don Luis de Unzaga, chose to cooperate with the locals. He invited French residents to serve in government and convinced them they could work with their Spanish rulers. New Orleans was a thriving city. More and more goods were shipped to the enormous warehouses, and more ships arrived to do business. Life for everyone in Louisiana could be prosperous and agreeable under the Spanish flag.

Across the river, the British had their own troubles. Upstart subjects in the Atlantic colonies rumbled about rebellion, war, and even independence. This was good for Spain. If England had distractions to the east, it would not venture into Louisiana.

In 1775, a letter arrived on Unzaga's desk from an American general, Charles Lee. He asked the governor's assistance in a rebellion against the British. The Revolutionary War had begun.

The Louisiana Purchase

The Battle of Lexington in 1775 marked the beginning of the American Revolution.

Chapter 4

The last boat of British troops leaves New York in 1783.

The Shifting Balance of Power

In 1783, the Americans defeated the British. Spain had aided the Patriots by securing the port of New Orleans. Only American, French, and Spanish ships were allowed on the Mississippi River.

The Louisiana Purchase

Spain and the United States were now neighbors. In the 1783 Treaty of Paris, England gave up not only its colonies along the Atlantic but also the inland frontier stretching to the Mississippi. The Americans were on the east bank of the Mississippi River, the Spanish on the west. England also returned East and West Florida to Spain, giving Spain command of the entire Gulf of Mexico.

> **Renewed New Orleans**
>
> In 1788 and again in 1794, New Orleans almost completely burned to the ground. Both times, though, the city rebuilt bigger and more beautiful than before.

Another important clause of the treaty allowed the Americans free access to the Mississippi River. Though the river officially fell under Spanish rule, Americans received permanent rights to navigate its waters. In addition, the Spanish gave American merchants the Right of Deposit in New Orleans which allowed the merchants to store and move their goods through the port without taxation.

Trouble Between Neighbors

Its new neighbor immediately troubled Spain, however. After the war, thousands of Americans arrived in the frontier. American traders ignored Spanish regulations, smuggling gold and silver into the United States. Officials in New Orleans grew angry as

Americans profited handsomely while the Spaniards received no taxes. By 1784, Spain closed off free access to the Lower Mississippi territory, the area south of the Missouri River. If Americans wanted to move their goods, they would have to pay just like anyone else.

The settlers were furious. Some demanded war against Spain. Others gave in, moved across the river, and became Spanish citizens. A few even argued that the frontier should secede from the United States. That way they could form their own country and negotiate new terms with Spain.

Meanwhile, the young American government had little capacity to deal with any outside troubles. It had enough problems of its own trying to move ahead as a new nation. A central government had to be formed. Laws had to be created and agreed upon. The future of the West would move forward, but slowly.

As debates, arguments, and visions for the future of the country carried on, two political parties took shape. Each took a different view as to what role the new

Conflicting Views

Early U.S. presidential elections worked differently than they do today. At that time, the candidate who received the most votes became president, and the one who came in second became vice president.

John Adams was only narrowly elected president in December 1796 and his opponent, Thomas Jefferson, became vice president. The two men held opposite views. The conflicts between them led to the formation of two political parties—the Federalists (Adams) and the Republicans (Jefferson).

The Louisiana Purchase

John Adams

central government should take in the workings of the nation. The Federalists, led by Alexander Hamilton and John Adams, favored a strong central, federal government. The Republicans, led by Thomas Jefferson, believed in a weaker central system with more power kept in the hands of the states. Both parties agreed on another key issue, however. They supported western expansion, knowing the value of the rich land.

Meanwhile, the European powers soon returned to war. England and France struggled for control of the Atlantic. The Federalists favored England, while the Republicans wanted to side with their old ally, France. Some in the middle, including the first U.S. president, George Washington, took a third view: neutrality. Hoping to keep their fledgling nation out of costly trouble, they insisted the United States side with neither nation.

Treaties and Secrets

The young United States tried to avoid the conflicts of the

A Secret Agent for Spain

James Wilkinson was a general in the Revolutionary War. But later, he became part of a conspiracy to replace General Washington as the commander of the Revolutionary Army. Wilkinson continued to serve but later resigned under accusations of corruption.

Wilkinson moved to Kentucky and suffered several failed business ventures. In 1787, he went to New Orleans to negotiate favorable trade relations for Kentucky on the Mississippi. He also swore allegiance to Spain and became their secret agent. When Kentucky negotiated to separate from Virginia, Wilkinson argued that Kentucky should consider becoming a part of Spain. The Spanish governors in New Orleans paid Wilkinson to encourage Americans to settle near Louisiana and join the colony as Spanish citizens.

Still believed loyal to the United States, Wilkinson returned to the U.S. army as a general. Not knowing Wilkinson's secret life, Jefferson assigned him to lead the army to invade New Orleans and fight the French over Louisiana if needed. Despite his secret efforts, Wilkinson stood as an American general the day the French turned Louisiana over to the United States.

The Louisiana Purchase

Europeans, but neutrality was impossible.

In 1789, France fell into a revolution of its own. Radicals destroyed the monarchy. King Louis XVI and members of royalty were beheaded. In their place, a stream of revolutionary leaders followed, each struggling for control of the government.

During the French Revolution, the British and French battled for control of the Atlantic Ocean. In the process, both navies captured dozens of American ships and their crews. This unjust practice was disastrous for U.S. trade, and it raised the fury of both American political parties.

In 1793, Edmond Charles Èdouard Genêt arrived as France's minister to the United States. One of his primary assignments—a secret one—was to raise an army in Louisiana and overthrow the Spanish government. He had orders to commission Americans as officers in the secret army.

The plan also called for him to capture British and Spanish ships and arm them for an attack on New Orleans. The Spanish discovered

War Called Off

In 1793, with the Lower Mississippi still closed, the United States considered an invasion to take Louisiana from Spain. An army led by General George Rogers Clark prepared to attack, but the plan was called off.

John Jay

France's plot and warned President Washington. The discovery greatly embarrassed France. Genêt was fired, and the French government backed down regarding Louisiana—at least for the moment.

In 1794, President Washington sought to build a better peace with England. He sent John Jay, a Federalist, to negotiate a new treaty. Jay returned with

The Louisiana Purchase

numerous agreements, including that British troops leave the Northwest territory. The Jay Treaty also promised good trade relations with England and tried to retain the American goal of neutrality.

The Federalist-backed treaty outraged Republicans. They called Jay a traitor and claimed he had pushed the nation to the side of England. Jefferson said the treaty would offend France. His warning soon proved correct.

The French immediately declared the treaty an act of aggression. They said the United States had broken allegiance with them. In response, the French stepped up their attacks at sea, capturing hundreds of U.S. ships. Again, Americans called for war. But John Adams, who was elected president in 1796, resisted making an outright declaration. Instead, Congress granted President Adams authority to increase the size of the U.S. Navy, sending warships off to protect the country's merchant vessels. Though it was an undeclared war, by 1798 it was war all the same. Trying to keep a sense of neutrality, the Americans called it the Quasi War (quasi means partial or less than fully real). Tensions between the old allies were high.

France created problems on land as well. Ever since Louis XV gave Louisiana to Spain in 1762, France vowed to get it back. England had land in the north, while Spain controlled territory to the south. To its great disgrace, France had nothing. Leaders of the French Republic demanded its return.

Not surprisingly, Spain saw its situation as even worse than before the American Revolution. The United States seemed just as threatening as England. Thousands of American settlers now lived in the frontier. They traveled in and out of Spanish Louisiana. Spain even invited Americans to settle in Louisiana and become citizens of Spain. Like the French locals, however, the settlers seldom gave up their loyalty to their native country.

Thomas Jefferson was Secretary of State from 1790 to 1793, and he supported the migration of Americans to Spanish territory. In his vision, Spain eventually would give up Louisiana to the United States, either by treaty or by force. In a letter to President Washington, Jefferson wrote,

> *I wish a hundred thousand of our inhabitants would accept the invitation. ... It will be the means to deliver to us peaceably what may otherwise cost a war.*[1]

The Jay Treaty of 1794 also upset the Spanish. Like the French, they believed the United States and England had forged an alliance. Spanish leaders feared

The Louisiana Purchase

the Americans would support a British invasion into Louisiana, and the two would divide the territory between themselves.

Spain's fears grew even worse when they discovered the French plot to regain Louisiana. France was a mighty power. It controlled much of the Caribbean, rivaling Spain's influence in the region. Also, France's armies were making great gains in Europe under a brilliant young general named Napoleon Bonaparte. The Spanish realized they stood alone, their frontier weak to potential invaders.

Out of concern for their holdings, the Spanish took a new, sudden interest in Louisiana. Governors in the territory sent explorers into the region, encouraged colonization by Spanish citizens, and opened the area to greater Spanish trade, all in hopes of strengthening their grip and keeping other countries at bay. King Charles IV of Spain also sought alliance with the United States.

In 1795, Spain agreed to a new treaty, which reopened the Lower Mississippi territory to American trade. To the Spanish, the agreement was known as the Treaty of San Lorenzo, after the city in Spain where it was signed on October 27. Americans called it Pinckney's Treaty, after the chief U.S. negotiator.

Most importantly, the treaty restored the Right of Deposit. Americans could again trade freely in New Orleans. Spain also agreed to a new boundary line for the Floridas, giving more land to the United States and less to Spain. In 1798, Congress declared the new region the Mississippi Territory.

Both Spain and the United States were satisfied with their treaty. The United States gained renewed access to New Orleans, and the Spanish were confident that Louisiana was safe from any American claims. Jefferson later wrote,

> Spain might have retained [New Orleans] quietly for years. Her pacific dispositions, her feeble state, would induce her to increase our facilities there, so that her possession of the place would be hardly felt by us.[2]

Unfortunately for both nations, however, the French had other plans.

Trail of Tears

During American settlement of the frontier beyond the Appalachians, Native American tribes were continually forced westward. Their territories became smaller and smaller, either by gunpoint or by treaty—but usually under threat of force. By the 1830s, the five major tribes in the southeast were forcibly pushed west of the Mississippi River. Their journey over thousands of miles became known as the "Trail of Tears."

The Louisiana Purchase

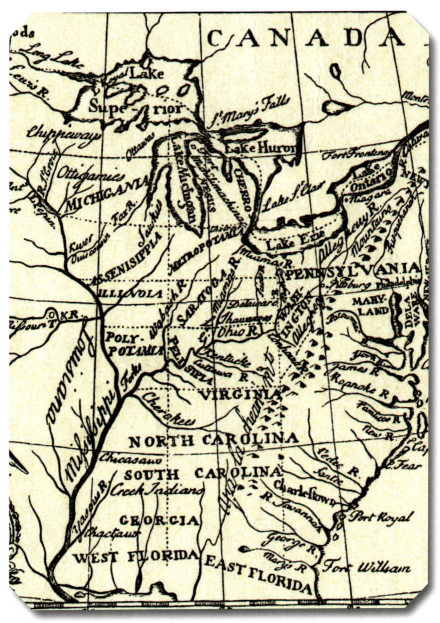

The first map to show the division of the western territories as suggested by Jefferson

Chapter 5

Napoleon defeats the British at Toulon in southern France, 1793

Napoleon's Vision of Empire

The French Revolution, which began in 1789, continued for ten bloody years. During that decade, chaos ruled in France's government. Rival leaders rose to power through violence and murder, only to later fall to the same fate themselves. Foreign

The Louisiana Purchase

negotiators would make an agreement with one French official, then return months later to find him imprisoned. Terror, corruption, and strife exhausted the French people.

A Leader Emerges

One man emerged whose brilliance and leadership made him a hero and restored the nation—Napoleon Bonaparte. For three years, the young general had led his troops to numerous victories, winning land in Italy and pushing back the Austrian Empire to the east. In October 1799, at the age of 30, Napoleon returned to Paris as a hero wanting political power.

The ambitious general had long desired to rule the nation. On November 9, his forces overthrew the Directory, which was the group running the government, and Napoleon seized power. Napoleon set up a new government under three leaders, known as Consuls. The general took the title "First Consul," becoming a sole ruler, while the other two consuls faded into minor posts.

Bonaparte's Brothers

Napoleon Bonaparte had two brothers, Lucien and Joseph. They were given important roles in government when Napoleon took over. The brothers would later oppose the Louisiana Purchase.

Napoleon swiftly brought the country to order, establishing peace and rebuilding the government under his strict rule. He also planned to return France to its place among European powers and as the most powerful nation on Earth. He poured resources into growing a mighty army. He added warships at sea. He extended his grip on lands in Italy and Germany.

He also plotted to reestablish France in the New World. The loss of Louisiana to Spain had been a sore spot for the French. Within months of coming to power, Napoleon devised a plan to regain the lost colony.

Napoleon Bonaparte

Napoleon Bonaparte was born on the isle of Corsica in the Mediterranean in 1769. He attended the Paris Military Academy and became a lieutenant at 16. Even as a young man, he was respected for his military genius.

By 1797, he had become a French general and a hero. France had suffered through years of internal revolution and saw Napoleon as a leader who could save the nation.

In November 1799, after ten years of revolution, Napoleon returned to Paris and overthrew the government. Established as First Consul, Napoleon ruled as a dictator. By 1804, Napoleon pressured the government to accept him as Emperor of France for life. For the next eight years, Napoleon fought his way across Europe. He captured territory all the way to Russia where the enemy pushed his armies back to France. Other nations drove Napoleon to eventual defeat and forced him to give up his throne in April 1814.

In March 1815, Napoleon escaped from his forced exile and raised an army to regain control. After 100 days of fighting, he was defeated at the Battle of Waterloo.

He died in exile in 1821 on the tiny island of St. Helena, far from his French homeland.

The Louisiana Purchase

A Secret Offer

In the summer of 1800, Napoleon secretly sent an offer to King Charles IV of Spain. France would generously give Etruria, a wealthy and recently captured kingdom in northern Italy, in exchange for Spain's holdings in Louisiana.

Charles IV had little interest in the wilderness north of Mexico, except as a buffer between the Americans and his rich silver and gold mines in the south. The Spanish king also feared the determined and powerful Napoleon. What the French general did not achieve by negotiation, he often took by force. Attack on Louisiana was just as possible from the newly strengthened French army as it was from American or British forces. For the moment, though, Napoleon offered a peaceful treaty and a land exchange.

Just as important, Charles IV's ambitious wife, Queen María Luísa, was delighted by the offer. She was the deciding voice in Spanish rule. Charles IV was a weak leader, while María Luísa was intelligent and cunning. Spain did not need Louisiana, she reasoned, as it already had vast holdings in the New World. She saw Etruria as an opportunity to expand Spain's influence in Europe. Etruria would also serve as a throne for her namesake daughter, María Luísa. The young princess

Napoleon planning a battle

was newly married, and she and her husband would soon rule a kingdom known for its riches and influence in the region.

Between the fear of Napoleon and the excitement over the offer of Etruria, Spain accepted Napoleon's proposal. They even agreed to deliver six valuable Spanish warships to the French navy.

Napoleon was pleased as well. He asked for only one more thing—that the agreement remain a secret. He insisted that if either the Americans or British found

The Louisiana Purchase

out about the treaty, they would be upset. The United States might try to take over Louisiana before French forces could arrive. The British might send their powerful navy to capture New Orleans or attack down the Mississippi River from Canada. The Spanish agreed. Their weak military presence in the region would be no match for either enemy.

On October 1, 1800, French and Spanish representatives signed the secret Treaty of San Ildefonso. Without announcement or fanfare, the exchange was sealed. Napoleon's ambitious vision of conquest in the New World took a giant step forward.

> **A Puppet Ruler**
>
> One condition of the Treaty of San Ildefonso was that Etruria be recognized by other European nations under the rule of Charles IV's daughter María Luísa. Napoleon insisted that would happen, but years went by, and no nation agreed to accept the puppet ruler. Though the Spanish king and queen protested, they were too weak to stop Napoleon.

Another Troubling Rumor for Jefferson

Political secrets seldom remain secret. Within months of the signing, rumors of the Treaty of San Ildefonso spread to England and the United States.

Thomas Jefferson was inaugurated as president of the United States on March 4, 1801. Only two weeks earlier, he had survived an election filled with lies, accusations, personal attacks, and rumors.

Now he heard a rumor of secret negotiations. Spain might agree to turn over Louisiana and East and West Florida to France. Jefferson was shocked. Only months before, Napoleon had signed an agreement to close the Quasi War and establish peaceful relations with the United States. Jefferson did not know that just one day later, France and Spain had sealed the Treaty of San Ildefonso.

As long as Spain was in control, the U.S. position was strong. A French presence in Louisiana would be far different, however. Napoleon made no move without a purpose. French control of Louisiana could prove disastrous for the United States. Napoleon could shut down the Lower Mississippi, cripple trade in New Orleans, and cut off American expansion.

Timing was critical. If the rumors were true, French troops would soon march into New Orleans. Already, leaders in Congress cried out for war. Jefferson would later write to his friend Samuel du Pont,

> This little event, of France's possessing herself of Louisiana is the embryo of a tornado which will burst on the countries on both sides of the Atlantic and involve in its effects their highest destinies.[1]

The president knew he had to act.

The Louisiana Purchase

Ships at the mouth of the Mississippi River, late 1700s

Chapter 6

Thomas Jefferson

THE AMERICAN DILEMMA: JEFFERSON PURSUES PEACE

Americans were outraged that the Floridas, Louisiana, and especially New Orleans, might soon be in Napoleon's hands. They were unaware that the Florida territories were not part of the Treaty of San Ildefonso. Yet President Jefferson

The Louisiana Purchase

had few options. He feared war would be too costly and damaging to his young nation. Instead, he sought to negotiate a peaceful agreement. Napoleon might be convinced that compromise with the United States was better than conflict.

Secretly, Jefferson hoped other enemies would divert the First Consul from his plans for the Spanish territories. In a letter to his friend Dr. Joseph Priestly, Jefferson wrote,

> *I did not expect [Napoleon] would yield till a war took place between France and England, and my hope was to palliate and endure.*[1]

Jefferson knew the two rival powers were in constant conflict. Battles flared on the Atlantic and in the Mediterranean. Also, England was one of several nations fighting Napoleon for control of central Europe. If the United States could negotiate as a friendly nation, it might keep Napoleon at bay. Soon enough, Jefferson hoped, another war with England

An Opportunity for Britain?

The British knew that the Americans were trying to negotiate a purchase of New Orleans, and they feared that such a deal was not in their interest. The British held out hopes that if Napoleon took Louisiana and the Americans entered into war, the British would have their chance. They could eventually invade Louisiana and take over the colony. The British even offered Joseph Bonaparte a substantial bribe if he could convince his brother Napoleon to hold onto Louisiana.

would force Napoleon's attentions away from Louisiana and back to Europe.

Napoleon had concerns about British interference as well. In fact, Jefferson's assessment of the situation was almost perfect. Napoleon well understood his archenemy could foil his plans. By the time Jefferson entered the White House, though, the general had won a series of decisive victories in Europe, shattering the enemy alliance. England stood alone, while France grew stronger and bolder.

Still, in the summer of 1801, Napoleon had much to concern him at home and elsewhere. He had

> ### Thomas Jefferson
>
> Many consider Thomas Jefferson to be one of the most brilliant leaders in U.S. history. He was a statesman, philosopher, scientist, farmer, architect, and much more. At the age of 33, he wrote the Declaration of Independence and later led his fellow patriots to write the U.S. Constitution. His philosophy was based on the idea of individual rights—citizens should decide on laws and government. The Constitution, not a king, would guide the nation.
>
> In 1797, Jefferson was elected vice president under John Adams. In 1801, he defeated Adams to become the nation's third president.
>
> Jefferson believed in prosperity based on agriculture and natural resources. He viewed the west as a promise of rich land and growing national wealth. He encouraged westward settlement. He believed that one day the nation would extend to the Pacific Ocean.
>
> Jefferson won reelection in 1804 and continued to support western exploration and expansion. Throughout his presidency, he maintained peace and avoided the ongoing war between England and France. That success allowed his young nation to grow and prosper.

The Louisiana Purchase

to restore order in France and pursue colonial intrigues as far off as India and South America. There was also a slave rebellion in San Domingue. For the moment, Louisiana could be ignored. Napoleon was not in a hurry to stir up trouble. Better to leave Louisiana in the hands of the Spanish. The rumor remained a rumor.

Jefferson, however, could not ignore the situation. Too much was at stake in New Orleans. If the French cut off trade along the Mississippi River and revoked the Right of Deposit in the port city, it could ruin U.S. commerce and destroy any hopes for building the frontier. Dreams of western expansion were pointless without the vital port.

Rumor or not, no other matter was more pressing for Jefferson.

An Envoy to France

By the fall of 1801, the president devised a response. He assigned statesman Robert Livingston to go to Paris as minister to France. Livingston had served as secretary of foreign affairs at the end of the American Revolution. He also knew many prominent French leaders, including Napoleon's minister of finance, François de Barbé-Marbois.

French statesman Charles Maurice de Talleyrand

Jefferson's first goal was to keep U.S. interests safe in New Orleans. Keeping the Floridas out of French hands was key, too. Louisiana, the land west of the Mississippi, was less important. The American diplomat had to convince Napoleon that if France took the port city and the Spanish territories to the east, he would harm the relationship between France and the United States.

Livingston hoped to persuade the general to release the port—and the Floridas—to the United States. If the

The Louisiana Purchase

Americans controlled the territory, they would give the French safe harbor in the Gulf and free trade in New Orleans. If Napoleon declined, friendly terms between the two nations would end. Whatever his advances on the continent, the United States would stand opposed.

Livingston arrived at the port of L'Orient, France, on November 13, 1801. Within a month, he met with Charles Maurice de Talleyrand, France's Minister of Foreign Affairs. Talleyrand formally introduced Livingston to Napoleon on December 6. The diplomat quickly pressed his case, but Napoleon knew he had the upper hand. The Americans were not even sure if a deal for France to acquire Louisiana was in the works. Napoleon remained friendly but ignored Livingston's letters and pleas for consideration. Talleyrand repeatedly taunted the American. He hinted that

Talleyrand's Sordid Pursuits

Charles Maurice de Talleyrand, Napoleon's foreign minister, had a long history of corruption and deceit. He came from an aristocratic family and had worked under King Louis XVI. He then allied himself with the rebels when the French Revolution broke out. Later, he followed Napoleon into power and rose to become one of his counselors. Talleyrand was later involved in a scandal known as the "XYZ Affair." He worked to force American diplomats to bribe French officials into ending the Quasi War. Rumors tied him to kidnappings and murders, and he eventually became a secret agent to Tsar Alexander of Russia against Napoleon.

James Madison

France and Spain were in discussions but had not reached an agreement.

The combination of arrogance and denials made Livingston furious. Everywhere he turned, he came up empty. Barbé-Marbois could not help nor could his old friend from the American Revolution, the great General Lafayette. The only thing clear about Talleyrand was his rudeness.

The Louisiana Purchase

Livingston even befriended Napoleon's older brother, Joseph, but this proved to be a dead end as well. Whenever the question of Louisiana came up, Joseph admitted he had no influence over his brother. After several weeks, Livingston angrily complained in a letter to James Madison, the U.S. Secretary of State:

> *There never was a government in which less could be done by negotiation than here. There is no people, no legislature, no counselors. One man is everything. He seldom asks advice, and never hears it unasked. His ministers are mere clerks; and his legislature and counselor parade officers.*[2]

Though frustrated, Livingston still believed he could fulfill his president's orders. He just needed more time. Meanwhile, the ruler of France embarked on his own timetable.

Napoleon's Plan Unfolds

On November 22, 1801, just nine days after Livingston's arrival in Paris, a massive French army set sail for the New World. More than 28,500 troops made up the force.

Napoleon placed one of his most trusted generals in charge—his brother-in-law Charles Victor Emmanuel Leclerc. First, Leclerc would to sail to San Domingue.

A former slave named Toussaint L'Ouverture had led a successful slave rebellion and now controlled the entire island. Napoleon wanted L'Ouverture captured and order restored. As Napoleon wrote to his Foreign Minister, Talleyrand, "… it is for the benefit of civilization that this Algiers [L'Ouverture] in American waters be destroyed."[3] With such a powerful army, Leclerc was sure to quickly crush the rebellion.

Next, Leclerc and his army would sail across the Gulf of Mexico and march on New Orleans. Leclerc would have the honor of reestablishing France once again on the continent. Napoleon's advance on North America was about to begin.

The Louisiana Purchase

Napoleon Bonaparte

Chapter 7

People in London celebrate peace with France.

The Twists of Fate

Leclerc arrived in San Domingue on January 29, 1802. His forces would dispose of L'Ouverture within a month or two, perhaps only a few weeks. Then, he would lead an army to New Orleans. Between rumors and spies, Livingston soon

The Louisiana Purchase

learned of Napoleon's secret plan. By April, Secretary of State Madison received Livingston's letter warning that an estimated 5,000 to 7,000 troops would move on Louisiana as a lead force.

Growing Desperation

President Jefferson faced a situation growing worse by the day. Negotiations had failed and an army of French troops made port just 1,300 miles (2,100 km) from Louisiana. To make matters worse, Napoleon had just signed the Treaty of Amiens, establishing a fragile peace with the British. Jefferson still believed that, with the right incentive, he could convince Napoleon to give up on his plans. Jefferson saw two choices, neither of them good, but better than French occupation in New Orleans.

The United States might still reach a peaceful settlement if it offered to purchase New Orleans and the Floridas. Napoleon needed money to fund his many adventures around the globe. Building an army and navy cost a fortune. Cash might entice the general to turn his ambitions elsewhere.

But if Napoleon refused to agree, Jefferson had one last resort—war. Yet even then, the president knew that fighting France without an ally would likely end in defeat. Only by siding with its old enemy, England, might the United States succeed.

In response to Livingston's letter, Madison sent orders to pursue a purchase. Napoleon could name his price for New Orleans and East and West Florida.

Jefferson also wrote to Livingston, explaining the likelihood of all-out conflict. The president wanted Livingston to pursue peace, but threaten war. Perhaps just knowing that England could join the conflict would be enough to drive Napoleon to the bargaining table.

Jefferson called on his close friend, Pierre S. du Pont de Nemours, to go to Livingston. Du Pont had influence in Paris. Perhaps he, too, could

> **Robert Livingston**
>
> Robert Livingston was a leader throughout the American Revolution. He was a close friend of Thomas Jefferson and helped him draft the Declaration of Independence. He later led his home state, New York, to ratify the Constitution.
>
> Livingston was born to a prominent New York family in 1746. He became an early member of the Sons of Liberty in New York, a group of patriots that helped to gain support for the coming revolution. He served as secretary of state until 1783, after which he led his state as chancellor (governor). In 1789, he administered the presidential oath of office to George Washington.
>
> After the signing of the Louisiana Purchase, Livingston continued to serve as minister to France until 1805. When he returned to the United States, he again became active in New York politics and supported several prosperous business ventures. An enthusiastic scientist, he worked with Robert Fulton to develop the first steamboat, a revolution in improving transportation.

The Louisiana Purchase

convince the French to reconsider. He carried a letter from Jefferson, dated April 18, 1802, which stated:

> There is on the globe one single spot, the possessor of which is our natural and habitual enemy. It is New Orleans. ... The day that France takes possession of New Orleans, fixes the sentence, which is to restrain her forever within her low-watermark. It seals the union of two nations, who, in conjunction, can maintain exclusive possession of the ocean. From that moment, we must marry ourselves to the British fleet and nation.
>
> This is not a state of things we seek or desire. It is one which this measure, if adopted by France, forces on us as necessarily, as any other cause, by the laws of nature, brings on its necessary effect.[1]

Jefferson's words were forceful and clear. He may have intended it to be shared directly with Napoleon. A few pages later, he reminded Livingston that a peaceful solution remained:

> If France considers Louisiana, however, as indispensable for her views, she might perhaps be willing to look about for arrangements which might reconcile it to our interests. If anything could do this, it would be the ceding to us the island of New Orleans and the Floridas.[2]

Toussaint L'Ouverture

Livingston renewed his efforts to persuade Napoleon. The American diplomat pressured his contacts again and wrote an essay in which he made dozens of arguments against colonization by the French. Copies were sent to Napoleon and his close advisors.

Napoleon refused all persuasion. In April, he had already appointed a governor for Louisiana, General

The Louisiana Purchase

Claude Victor. He then ordered Victor and Admiral Denis Decrès to organize a force for the takeover of Louisiana. Napoleon again demanded secrecy, wanting to throw off the Americans and British. He wrote to Decrès, "It is our intention to take Louisiana as soon as possible; and that the expedition take place in the greatest secrecy."[3] Decrès gathered 12 ships while General Victor sought 3,000 men. The force would set sail by September.

Devastation in San Domingue

When General Leclerc arrived at Port-au-Prince, an important port in San Domingue, he found that nearly the entire city had been burned to the ground by rebels. Rebels also had destroyed Cap Haitien, a second port city. Toussaint L'Ouverture waited in the wilderness, preparing for an aggressive guerilla war. His soldiers left behind the bodies of white settlers, poisoned wells, and destroyed plantations.

Another Conqueror

Toussaint L'Ouverture was born a slave on San Domingue, like hundreds of thousands of blacks on the French colony. A local priest recognized the boy's intelligence and taught him to read and write, breaking colony law.

When the slaves rebelled in 1791, Toussaint emerged as a leader. He said a vision of a black Madonna told him he would lead the slave rebellion to victory. He took the name L'Ouverture, meaning "opening," to impress upon followers that he could guide them to self-rule.

After his capture in June 1802, L'Ouverture was taken to France and imprisoned. He died there in April 1803.

Essential Events

> **Yellow Fever**
>
> Yellow Fever is a virus, most commonly transported by mosquitoes. The name comes from the yellowing of the skin while the disease is present. The infection can be life-threatening. Though vaccines have done away with yellow fever in most of the world, outbreaks still occur in remote areas and developing nations in Africa and Central and South America.

Leclerc's troops faced ambushes, sniper attacks, and hand-to-hand combat. Months dragged on, and L'Ouverture kept the French at bay.

Spring brought yellow fever. Locals were immune to the disease, but French troops were not. Within weeks, half of Leclerc's forces were sick or dead. In June, Leclerc captured L'Ouverture by tricking him into a truce. However, Leclerc's troubles only grew worse. Reacting to their leader's capture, the guerilla army attacked in full force. Then, news spread that Napoleon planned to restore slavery on the island. With that, a half million former slaves joined the battle against Leclerc.

The situation was more alarming by September. Leclerc wrote to Napoleon that he desperately needed more troops. After starting with more than 28,000 men, only 4,000 active soldiers were left. Without reinforcements, warned Leclerc, San Domingue "will be forever lost to France."[4] However, it would take another month for his letter to reach Paris.

The Louisiana Purchase

"Envoy Extraordinary"

In the United States, reports arrived of a French fleet preparing to sail from Holland to Louisiana. Americans believed troops also would soon embark from San Domingue. The truth of Leclerc's troubles had not yet reached the rest of the world. Jefferson only knew his time and options were running out. The problem then turned into a major crisis.

The Spanish cancelled the U.S. Right of Deposit in New Orleans on a secret order from King Charles IV. On October 16, 1802, American shipping through the port of New Orleans ceased.

Frontiersmen responded with a petition to the government in Washington City:

> *The Mississippi is ours by the law of nature. ... Our innumerable rivers swell its volume, and flow with it to the Gulf of Mexico. Its mouth is the only issue which nature has given to our waters. ... No power in the world shall deprive us of this right.*[5]

In Congress, Senator James Ross of Pennsylvania drafted a call for the president to raise an army and seize New Orleans before the French arrived. However, Jefferson convinced Congress that negotiation could still win out. Encouraging rumors arrived that England

and France were on the verge of war, just as the president had predicted. Congress agreed to follow Jefferson's lead.

In January 1803, Jefferson asked James Monroe to go to Napoleon and press the American case. Monroe had been minister to France. Perhaps working with Livingston, they could reach a breakthrough. Monroe, Jefferson, and Madison planned a strategy. On March 8, the newly titled "Envoy Extraordinary," Monroe, sailed for France.

Shattered Plans

Meanwhile, Leclerc's letter sent Napoleon into a rage. L'Ouverture had been a thorn in his side for years. Now rebellious slaves had upset his plans again. Still, Napoleon's plans for empire had to go forward.

Napoleon ordered General Jean-Baptiste Rochambeau to relieve Leclerc. By the time Admiral Decrès had more troops and weapons, winter had arrived. Ice blocked his ships, freezing them into port. Decrès and his troops would not be able to leave until spring. In January 1803, news arrived that yellow fever had taken Leclerc. His army of 30,000 men lay in ruins. Napoleon was so infuriated, he shouted, "Damn sugar, damn coffee, damn colonies."[6]

The Louisiana Purchase

James Monroe

Chapter 8

A closed volume containing the Louisiana Purchase, signed on April 30, 1803

The Louisiana Purchase

James Monroe arrived in Paris on April 12, 1803—the last chance for American diplomacy. If he could not convince Napoleon to agree to a settlement, the United States would ask for England's help and prepare for war.

The Louisiana Purchase

Monroe carried three offers from the president. First, the United States would try to purchase New Orleans and the Floridas. Jefferson authorized a sum of up to $10 million. If Napoleon refused, Monroe would offer to purchase only New Orleans. American trade could not survive without New Orleans. Third, if France again declined, Monroe would insist only that Americans retain the freedom to navigate the Mississippi and keep the Right of Deposit in New Orleans.

Jefferson had no desire for war. His third offer showed he was willing to accept French occupation if the general agreed to keep the port city and its river open and free to American merchants.

Jefferson's vision of his nation reaching the Pacific would have to wait. But he was convinced he would not have to wait long. Even if French forces moved into Louisiana and the

James Monroe

James Monroe served during the Revolutionary War and suffered serious wounds during a major battle. After the war, he returned to Virginia, where he became a close friend of Thomas Jefferson. Monroe served in the U.S. Senate and later as governor of Virginia.

After serving as "Envoy Extraordinary" for the Louisiana Purchase, Monroe went to England as the American minister. President Madison appointed him secretary of state in 1812. In 1814, Monroe doubled his posts, serving also as secretary of war (during the War of 1812 against the British).

Monroe was elected president in 1816. As president, he oversaw more western expansion and the secession of Florida by Spain to the United States in 1819. He served two terms as president. Like Jefferson and Adams before him, Monroe died on July 4th. The year was 1831.

Floridas, Napoleon would be distracted elsewhere. He had plans for European conquest—surely more important than capturing the wilderness of Louisiana. Besides, England would never stand for Napoleon's ambitions in the New World. The two rivals were on the verge of war again. Jefferson reasoned the Treaty of Amiens would never last. Napoleon would need all of his forces on the battlefields of Italy, Egypt, or Holland. He would abandon his plans for New Orleans. Jefferson hoped Louisiana stood as the least of the general's ambitions.

Jefferson believed the Americans and French could reach an agreement.

> **Napoleon's Temper**
>
> When Napoleon announced he was considering the sale of Louisiana, Foreign Minister Talleyrand rushed to Lucien and Joseph Bonaparte. He hoped they could convince the First Consul to change his mind. On April 7, 1803, the two brothers dared to interrupt Napoleon while he was in his bathtub.
>
> They began talking of trivial things and begging Napoleon's pardon for their sudden appearance. Soon, talk turned to Louisiana. They began lecturing their brother that he was making a terrible mistake. Joseph announced he would stir up opposition to block the sale.
>
> Napoleon, known for his short temper, became furious. At one moment, he stood up. Then he threw himself back into the tub, splashing water over his brothers. One of the servants in the room fainted, and others had to carry him off. Yet Napoleon's rage had just begun. He stood up again, grabbed his jeweled snuffbox, and smashed it to bits on the floor—driving his brothers from the room. That ended their efforts to influence his decision.

The Louisiana Purchase

Still, Monroe carried one more order. If Napoleon turned down all offers, the diplomat would leave France and go directly to England to press for an alliance with Britain.

The Tide Continues to Rise

Rumors had spread that Victor and Decrès had secret orders to invade England. In response, a massive British fleet sailed for Holland and set up a blockade. Should Decrès try to leave port, the British would attack. The French admiral knew he did not stand a chance against a more battle-ready enemy.

On San Domingue, Rochambeau suffered defeat after defeat. Between yellow fever and 500,000 angry former slaves, his plan for swift attack quickly turned to defense. Letters to Napoleon described a campaign in shambles.

Napoleon had already lost one army. Another remained trapped in Holland. The ongoing struggle for San Domingue locked up 30,000 more troops in a fight that could last for months. The British were on the verge of returning to war in Europe and Egypt. Napoleon needed every French soldier and money to fund the fight. Louisiana was becoming a dead end, and Napoleon knew it.

By April 1803, despite the protests of his brothers and Talleyrand, Napoleon decided to sell Louisiana to the Americans. He could no longer hold on to Louisiana, and he wanted to keep it out of British hands. His only choice was to cede it and the port of New Orleans to the United States. It was time to draw up plans. He explained,

> *They [the English] shall not have the Mississippi ... I have not a moment to lose in putting it out of their reach. I think of ceding it to the United States. ... to those republicans whose friendship I seek. ... and it appears to me that in the hands of this growing power, it will be more useful to the ... commerce of France than if I should try to keep it.*[1]

The next day, Napoleon announced his decision as final: "I renounce Louisiana. I renounce it with the greatest regret. To attempt obstinately to retain it would be folly."[2] Napoleon instructed Talleyrand to approach Livingston with the offer.

Louisiana?

Livingston sat facing the French foreign minister, barely able to speak. Neither he nor the president had considered an offer to buy the entire territory of Louisiana. Their goal was New Orleans and the

The Louisiana Purchase

Floridas. The Americans still did not know that the Floridas were not Napoleon's to sell.

The whole of Louisiana was an enticing idea. It included New Orleans and the entire length of the Mississippi River. The United States would control both banks and the port. And there was more—an imposing wilderness larger than the entire nation. Livingston could not be sure. He departed without giving Talleyrand an answer.

Livingston soon realized that Louisiana held incredible promise. After 14 months, he was on the brink of reaching a settlement—and without Monroe. He sent a note to Talleyrand requesting an immediate meeting. He had only a day before Monroe's arrival, and he wanted the offer in writing. Unfortunately, Talleyrand did not respond.

The Offer

Monroe arrived on April 12. Livingston still had no word from Talleyrand. The next day came without further news. That evening, Barbé-Marbois requested Livingston to come to the finance minister's office to discuss an urgent matter.

When the two men met, Barbé-Marbois explained that the offer had come directly from Napoleon.

Essential Events

François Barbé-Marbois

François Barbé-Marbois was an intelligent negotiator whose agreeable nature won him many an argument. He had served as a diplomat in Philadelphia during the 1780s and married an American.

At the outset of the French Revolution, he supported the royalty, which soon meant exile as the opposition rose to power. When Napoleon came to power, he freed Barbé-Marbois and gave him a place of prominence among his counselors.

After the Louisiana Purchase, Barbé-Marbois continued to hold a place of power, becoming a grand officer of the "Legion of Honor." His place of prominence helped him to keep his offices after Napoleon was later forced from power.

All of Louisiana, including New Orleans, was for sale at a price of $22.5 million.

Livingston said the United States could not afford such a price. Barbé-Marbois suggested that Livingston make a reasonable counter offer. Most importantly, the two sides should come to terms as quickly as possible.

Livingston returned to his desk and wrote to Secretary Madison:

> We shall do all we can to cheapen the purchase, but my present sentiment is that we shall buy[.][1]

Negotiation

The next morning, Livingston explained the situation to Monroe, who agreed to pursue the deal without a response from their president. Two weeks of negotiations still did not yield a deal. Finally, on April 30, an agreement was reached: $15 million. The sale of Louisiana would soon be complete.

The Louisiana Purchase

Talleyrand, Livingston, and Monroe

Chapter 9

Map of the United States in 1803, showing the Louisiana Purchase

THE NATION DOUBLES IN SIZE OVERNIGHT

With a price agreed upon, the French drafted a hasty three-page agreement within a day of settling the sum. On May 1, 1803, Napoleon officially accepted the terms. On May 2,

The Louisiana Purchase

Livingston, Monroe, and Barbé-Marbois signed the draft treaty. The United States had agreed to the largest land deal in history, doubling its size.

The Terms

The treaty described the conditions of the sale and rules to govern how the territory would be exchanged. The financial arrangement had two parts. First, the United States would pay $11.25 million in cash to France. Second, all debts from France to the United States would be cancelled, and any French debts to American citizens would be taken over and paid by the U.S. government. The debts amounted to an additional $3.75 million. The two figures totalled $15 million. The treaty also provided that France and Spain would have free access to the port of New Orleans for 12 years. As it was under the Right of Deposit granted to Americans, French and Spanish merchants would trade without taxation or duties imposed by the territory's new owner. The agreement added that the United States would not grant this right to any other nation. Napoleon wanted the British left out of this privilege.

> **Four Cents an Acre**
> Because the Louisiana Territory was so huge, the United States paid about four cents an acre for the entire area.

Perhaps most important to Napoleon, he also demanded that the territory immediately become part of the United States. Article III of the treaty stated:

> The inhabitants of the ceded territory shall be incorporated in the Union of the United States and admitted as soon as possible according to the principles of the federal Constitution to the enjoyment of all these rights, advantages and immunities of citizens of the United States...[1]

With Louisiana as a U.S. territory, not a colony, Napoleon believed it would keep England from making any future deal to purchase all or part of the region.

Monroe and Livingston agreed to each of Napoleon's demands, even though word of the deal had not yet reached President Jefferson.

When the three negotiators signed and sealed the treaty, Livingston announced:

> We have lived long, but this is the noblest work of our whole lives. ... From this day the United States take their place among the powers of the first rank. ... The instruments which we have just signed will cause no tears to be shed...[2]

Jefferson's Victory

In early June, Livingston's letter finally reached Secretary Madison. He immediately took it to President

The Louisiana Purchase

Jefferson. This was the first word of a solution that had reached the United States. Three weeks later, on July 3, another letter arrived, this one confirming that Livingston and Monroe had successfully agreed to purchase the entire Louisiana territory. Jefferson's gamble had transformed into a stunning success.

Jefferson drafted an announcement for the press. It would be the most important announcement of his career. Just in time for Independence Day, the *National Intelligencer* reported the incredible event.

Supporters hailed the Louisiana Purchase as a historic achievement. On July 8, Harrison Smith, editor of the *Intelligencer*, recognized what the treaty could mean to the future of his nation:

Enormous Expansion

Only 27 years after the signing of the Declaration of Independence, the United States grew from the original 13 colonies all the way to the Rocky Mountains.

> ... By the cession of Louisiana, we shall preserve peace, and acquire a territory of great extent, fertility, and local importance.[3]

Smith believed that the United States would soon become an equal among world powers. The Louisiana Purchase placed his nation on the threshold of greatness.

Opposition

Not all Americans agreed with Smith. Though the Federalists held far fewer seats in Congress than Jefferson's Republicans, they still held influence among the people. If the president wanted his treaty, he would have to convince Congress to agree. According to the Constitution, any treaty needed approval from the Senate.

The Federalists feared the deal would cheapen land across the country. Reducing the value of property, they argued, would ruin people's holdings. Others argued the purchase would bankrupt the

---

Financing the Deal

The United States now owed France $15 million—money the U.S. government did not have. In fact, the U.S. government had more than $7 million of its own debts to pay.

Barbé-Marbois had an answer. Since French banks would need to finance Napoleon's war effort, the United States would have to turn to others to lend them the money. They approached two of Europe's most stable banks: London's Alexander Baring & Company and Amsterdam's Hope & Company. The companies worked together under the leadership of Alexander Baring in London, agreeing to issue bonds, which the United States would pay back with 6 percent interest. Each bank would eventually earn at least $3 million on the loans.

Baring had to request approval from the British government. Surprisingly, Parliament agreed. England had declared war on France on May 18, 1803. However, the British still feared a French presence in Louisiana. They wanted to keep Napoleon's troops and ships from causing trouble in the West, even if it meant funding his war effort in Europe. So, in a strange twist, England helped finance the Louisiana Purchase.

The Louisiana Purchase

nation. Senator Samuel White of Delaware claimed Louisiana "will be the greatest curse that could at present befall us."[4]

Most of the Federalists represented New England and the Northeast. They believed the purchase would expand power among the southern and new western states. Some in the party even wanted to break off from the rest of the nation.

Nation of New England?

Efforts by certain leaders in the northeast to break away from the Union did not end with the agreement to ratify the Louisiana Purchase. For some, the effort grew stronger. Later, during the War of 1812, many people of New England aided the British forces attacking from Canada.

Fortunately for Jefferson, the opposition's influence was small and their voices drowned out by the support from the rest of Congress and the nation.

However, the Federalists raised one last concern that was of major importance. They argued that the Constitution did not allow a president to purchase territory on behalf of the nation. In truth, they were correct.

The argument troubled Jefferson, who believed in a strict interpretation of the Constitution. Nevertheless, he carefully argued that the president's constitutional right to make treaties also included the right to purchase land.

The president argued vehemently that Congress must approve the treaty or face the threat of an invasion. Both France and England looked on Louisiana with visions of colonial expansion. Both nations could drag the United States into a long and costly war. Napoleon would not wait much longer. Jefferson called on Congress to ratify the treaty, as it was in the best interests of the nation.

Five months after Napoleon officially accepted the U.S. offer, the Senate took up the treaty at last. After four days in heated debate, on October 20, 1803, the Senate voted in favor of the Louisiana Purchase. All but one of the Federalist senators voted against it.

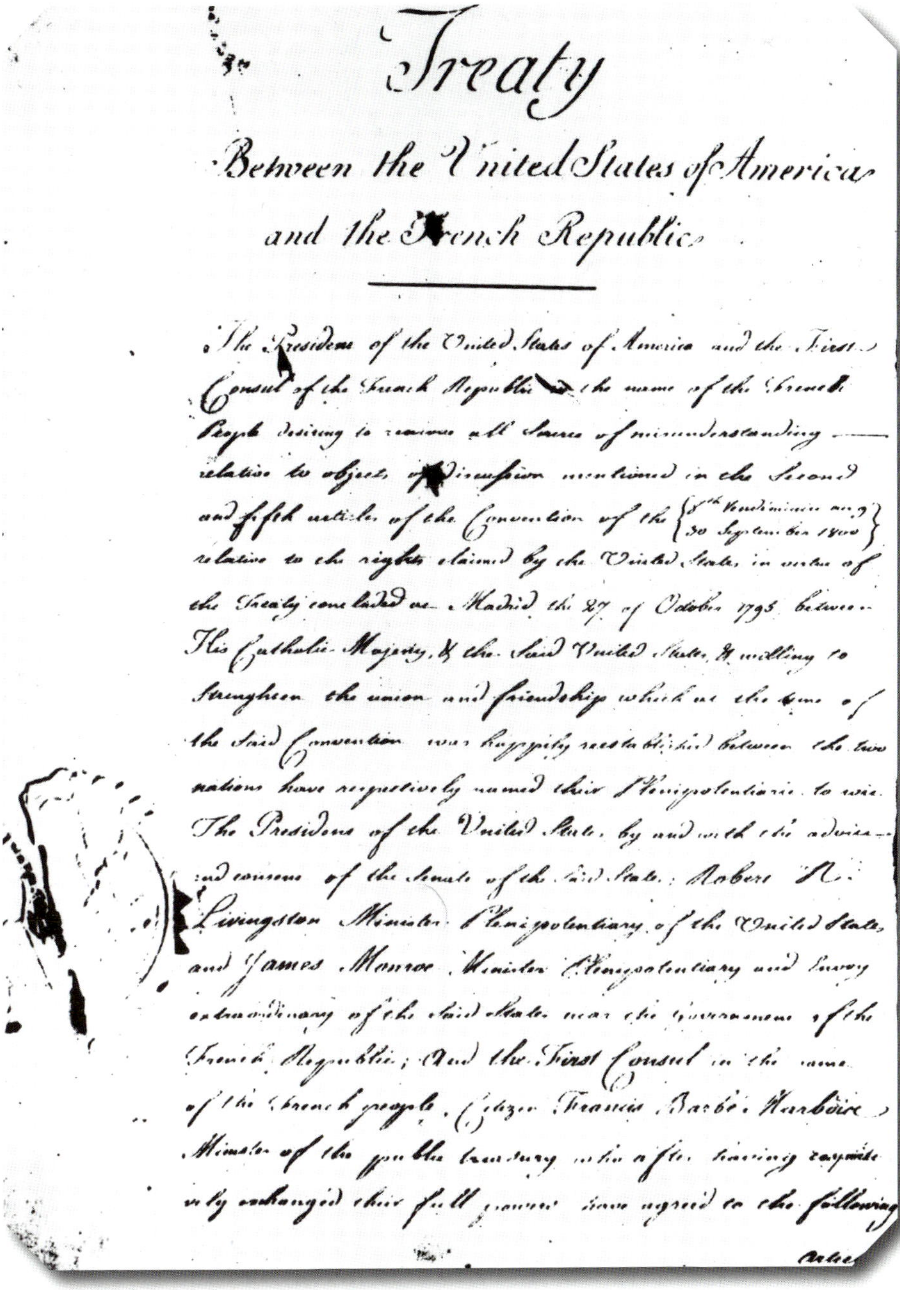

Treaty

Between the United States of America and the French Republic

The President of the United States of America and the First Consul of the French Republic in the name of the French People desiring to remove all Source of misunderstanding relative to objects of Discussion mentioned in the Second and fifth articles of the Convention of the {8th Vendémiaire an 9 / 30 September 1800} relative to the rights claimed by the United States in virtue of the Treaty concluded at Madrid the 27 of October 1795 between His Catholic Majesty & the said United States, & willing to Strengthen the union and friendship which at the time of the said Convention was happily reestablished between the two nations have respectively named their Plenipotentiaries to wit: The President of the United States, by and with the advice and consent of the Senate of the said States; Robert R. Livingston Minister Plenipotentiary of the United States and James Monroe Minister Plenipotentiary and Envoy extraordinary of the said States near the Government of the French Republic; And the First Consul in the name of the French people, Citizen Francis Barbé Marbois Minister of the public treasury who after having respectively exchanged their full powers have agreed to the following articles

Louisiana Purchase Treaty

Chapter 10

King Charles IV of Spain and his family

The New America

News of the Louisiana Purchase spread quickly. Frontier settlers no longer feared Spain shutting down the New Orleans port or French troops driving them out. They would finally rule the West.

The Louisiana Purchase

The news also made its way to Spain. King Charles IV and Queen María Luísa protested that Napoleon had tricked them. French troops still controlled Etruria while their daughter sat on a meaningless throne. Carlos Irujo, the Spanish minister to the United States, declared that Napoleon had given his verbal agreement that he would not resell the territory. Only Spain had the right to buy it back. The United States had no authority to its claims. Irujo threatened that Spain would defend New Orleans. Jefferson responded with threats of his own, using military might as a negotiating tool. He knew only a small Spanish force protected Louisiana. He believed, too, that Charles IV wanted to avoid war. Jefferson was right.

In New Orleans, news of the purchase confused city leaders. On March 26, 1803, Pierre Clément de Laussat had landed in the port to assume eventual French control of the city from Spain. In July, Laussat received new orders from Napoleon. He was to receive Louisiana from the Spanish as planned, then turn over the territory to American officials. Louisiana had been sold.

A Scientific Opportunity

As a man of science, Jefferson also wondered what great discoveries of nature lay in store. An expedition to the West was only one of many scientific inquiries Jefferson fostered. He believed, as did others, that many new species of animals and plants lay in the West. Jefferson was even among those who speculated that the explorers might find ancient wooly mammoths still roaming the Plains.

By November 23, General James Wilkinson and American troops set up camp outside the city of New Orleans. Per instructions, on November 30, troops lowered the Spanish flag and replaced it with the French colors. Laussat was given the keys to New Orleans' four gates and a French reign that would last no more than 20 days. William Claiborne, Jefferson's newly appointed governor of Louisiana, arrived. On December 20, the French governor Laussat announced an end to the brief French rule. The French flag was lowered and replaced with the U.S. flag.

Completing Western Expansion

After the Louisiana Purchase and the Lewis and Clark Expedition, American expansion continued westward for several decades. The Oregon Territory came into dispute between U.S. and British claims for several years. After a 30-year dispute, Britain and the United States signed a treaty establishing U.S. ownership of the territory that includes present-day Oregon, Washington, Idaho, and parts of Montana and Wyoming west of the Continental Divide.

Spain disputed the boundaries of western Louisiana for several years. American settlers in Texas drove out the Spanish in 1836 and established their own independent republic. Texas joined the United States in 1845.

The end of the Mexican-American War in 1848 resulted in pushing Spanish interests almost entirely out of present-day U.S. boundaries. The Treaty of Guadalupe Hidalgo gave the United States Utah, Nevada, California, and most of New Mexico, and Arizona. The Gadsden Treaty with Mexico completed the purchase of the rest of Arizona and New Mexico in 1853.

The Louisiana Purchase

An Era of New Discovery

In a single day, the United States doubled in size. Suddenly, the nation owned a vast expanse of land, yet almost no American had ever seen it.

President Jefferson had a vision. He saw a land rich in resources and opportunity. However, even the territory's boundaries were unclear. The Spanish and French had never come to terms over where Louisiana ended and Spanish lands to the west began. England's colony, Canada, lay to the north, but there were no clear boundary lines. Maps of the day offered no help. The region was a blank slate.

Jefferson understood this even before he received news of Napoleon's offer. In January 1803—before Louisiana was in U.S. hands—he secretly requested funding from Congress for an exploratory expedition into the unknown territory that both the French and British claimed. For 300 years, explorers had searched for a shorter route to the Pacific. If one existed through the Louisiana territory, the United States would have an incredible advantage in world trade. Congress granted $2,500 for a small expeditionary group. Jefferson

Florida at Last

Almost 20 years after the Louisiana Purchase, the United States successfully acquired East and West Florida from Spain. The United States purchased the territory that included Florida and portions of Mississippi and Alabama for $5 million.

turned to Captain Meriwether Lewis to lead the expedition.

By the summer of 1803, the Louisiana Purchase turned Lewis's expedition from a secret to a celebrated adventure. He asked William Clark to join the expedition. On May 14, 1804, Lewis and Clark began their trip up the Missouri River. They journeyed through the Great Plains and over the Rocky Mountains. They found the Columbia River and followed it all the way to the Pacific. Their journey became one of the most famous events in U.S. history and led to years of exploration and settlement. This expedition opened the West and the next phase of U.S. expansion—what Jefferson deemed as a "vast empire for liberty."[1]

The territory known as Louisiana offered rich soil, plentiful trapping, and vast timber ranges. Over time, Louisiana became all or part of 15 new states.

The territory became the great frontier. Settlers flocked to the West. They built farms and towns, suffering hard winters and rugged terrain. Americans could see a future that Jefferson, Livingston, and Monroe had described. The Louisiana Purchase offered a map to the future. It gave shape to possibility.

The Louisiana Purchase

Meriwether Lewis

Essential Events

Timeline

1682

Rene La Salle reaches the mouth of the Mississippi River and claims the land for France. He names it after King Louis XIV.

1762

King Louis XV secretly cedes the Louisiana territory west of the Mississippi River to Spain.

1763

France loses the French and Indian War to England. All of Louisiana east of the Mississippi River goes to the British.

1789

The French Revolution brings chaotic rule under several leaders.

1791

A slave rebellion erupts on the French colony of San Domingue (present-day Haiti).

1793

The French plot to regain Spanish Louisiana.

The Louisiana Purchase

1775–1783

During the Revolutionary War, France and Spain aid the American cause. By 1783, the Americans defeat the British.

1783

The Treaty of Paris recognizes the United States of America.

1784

Spain closes the lower Mississippi River to American traders.

1795

The Pinckney Treaty reestablishes the American Right of Deposit in New Orleans.

1797

The Quasi War breaks out between the United States and France. The undeclared war ends by treaty on September 30, 1800.

1799

Napoleon Bonaparte takes control of the French government, ending the French Revolution.

Essential Events

Timeline

1800
The secret Treaty of San Ildefonso returns Louisiana and New Orleans to French ownership.

1801
Robert Livingston is sent to France to negotiate the purchase of New Orleans and the Floridas.

1802
In April, Livingston warns Jefferson that a French army is secretly planning to take New Orleans.

1803
In April, Napoleon offers the Americans all of Louisiana, including New Orleans.

1803
An agreement for the Louisiana Purchase is signed on April 30.

1803
The Senate votes in favor of the Louisiana Purchase on October 20.

The Louisiana Purchase

1802
During the summer, Napoleon orders Admiral Denis Decrès to organize an army to take over Louisiana.

1802
French forces on San Domingue are defeated. The Spanish authority in New Orleans closes the port to American trade.

1803
In January, Jefferson requests $2,500 from Congress for a secret exploratory expedition into Louisiana.

1803
Spain officially transfers ownership of Louisiana to the French on November 20.

1803
Louisiana officially becomes a part of the United States of America on December 20.

1804
Meriwether Lewis and William Clark set out on the "Voyage of Discovery" to explore the Louisiana Territory on May 14.

Essential Facts

Date of Event

May 2, 1803

Place of Event

Paris, France

Key Players

❖ Thomas Jefferson (U.S. president)

❖ Robert Livingston (U.S. minister to France)

❖ James Monroe (U.S. "Envoy Extraordinary")

❖ Napoleon Bonaparte (emperor of France)

❖ François de Barbé-Marbois (finance minister for France)

The Louisiana Purchase

Highlights of Event

❖ On October 1, 1800, Napoleon of France and King Charles IV of Spain agreed to the Treaty of San Ildefonso. The secret treaty would return Louisiana and New Orleans to French ownership.

❖ During the summer of 1802, Napoleon ordeed Admiral Denis Decrès to organize an army to secretly prepare for an expedition to take over Louisiana. The party was delayed repeatedly and never made it to Louisiana. Meanwhile, French troops were engaged in fighting over San Domingue and were defeated by the fall of 1802.

❖ President Jefferson assigned Robert Livingston and James Monroe to negotiate the purchase of New Orleans because of its strategic importance at the mouth of the Mississippi River.

❖ In April 1803, Napoleon decided to end his plans for Louisiana and authorized Barbé-Marbois to negotiate the sale. The United States acquired the Louisiana territory from the French for $15 million on May 2, 1803.

❖ Louisiana became part of the United States. The Lewis and Clark expedition explored the territory.

Quote

This little event, of France's possessing herself of Louisiana is the embryo of a tornado which will burst on the countries on both sides of the Atlantic and involve in its effects their highest destinies." —*Thomas Jefferson*

Additional Resources

Selected Bibliography

Blumberg, Rhoda. *What's the Deal? Jefferson, Napoleon, and the Louisiana Purchase*. Washington D.C.: National Geographic Society, 1998.

Brecher, Frank. *Negotiating the Louisiana Purchase: Robert Livingston's Mission to France, 1801–1804*. Jefferson, NC: McFarland, 2006.

Commager, Henry Steele, and Milton Cantor, eds. *Documents of American History, Vol. 1*. Englewood Cliffs, NJ: Prentice-Hall, 1988.

Davenport, John. *Louisiana Territory*. Philadelphia: Chelsea House, 2005.

Hitchens, Christopher. *Thomas Jefferson: Author of America*. New York: Atlas Books, 2005.

Janin, Hunt. *Claiming the American Wilderness: International Rivalry in the Trans-Mississippi West, 1528-1803*. Jefferson, NC: McFarland, 2006.

"The Louisiana Purchase, 1803, The Treaty and Related Documents." The Avalon Project at Yale Law School. <http://www.yale.edu/lawweb/avalon/diplomacy/france/fr1803m.htm>.

Nelson, Sheila. *Thomas Jefferson's America: The Louisiana Purchase 1800–1811*. Philadelphia: Mason Crest, 2005.

Payment, Simone. *La Salle: Claiming the Mississippi River for France*. New York: Rosen, 2004.

Schaffer, David. *The Louisiana Purchase: The Deal of the Century that Doubled the Nation*. Berkeley Heights, NJ: MyReportLinks.com Books, 2006.

Further Reading

Blumberg, Rhoda. *What's the Deal? Jefferson, Napoleon, and the Louisiana Purchase*. Washington D.C.: National Geographic Society, 1998.

Davenport, John. *Louisiana Territory*. Philadelphia: Chelsea House, 2005.

The Louisiana Purchase

Nelson, Sheila. *Thomas Jefferson's America: The Louisiana Purchase 1800–1811.* Philadelphia: Mason Crest, 2005.

Schaffer, David. *The Louisiana Purchase: The Deal of the Century that Doubled the Nation.* Berkeley Heights, NJ: MyReportLinks.com Books, 2006.

Web Links

To learn more about the Louisiana Purchase, visit ABDO Publishing Company on the World Wide Web at **www.abdopublishing.com.** Web sites about the Louisiana Purchase are featured on our Book Links page. These links are routinely monitored and updated to provide the most current information available.

Places to Visit

Monticello the Home of Thomas Jefferson
Intersection of Route 53 and Route 20, Charlottesville, VA 22902
800-243-0743
www.monticello.org
Tour Jefferson's home, gardens, and plantation.

Louisiana State Museum
The Cabildo, 701 Chartres Street, New Orleans, LA 70116
800-568-6968
lsm.crt.state.la.us/cabex.htm
The museum contains artifacts and art reflecting Louisiana's history and culture.

Louisiana Historical Society
5801 St. Charles Avenue, New Orleans, LA 70115
504-866-3049
www.louisianahistoricalsociety.org
Lectures provide insight into Louisiana's history.

Glossary

ally
> A person, group, or nation that associates with another to reach a shared goal.

cede
> To give away or transfer ownership of property.

colony
> An area of land ruled by a distant nation.

coup
> A sudden, sometimes violent, overthrow of a ruling governor or government.

denounce
> Publicly expressed opinion against a person or action.

diplomat
> An official who represents his or her government to another nation; a diplomat negotiates agreements and delivers messages to the foreign government.

expedition
> An organized trip to a region to either explore or take over ownership of that location.

federal
> Relating to a centralized form of government responsible for making laws and maintaining order between individual states that make up a nation.

Federalist Party
> One of the two major political parties to form after the American Revolution; led by Alexander Hamilton and John Adams, the Federalists supported a strong central government.

The Louisiana Purchase

frontier
    A region that has none or very little human settlement.

guerilla
    A person who engages in irregular warfare tactics.

navigate
    To find one's way through open sea, space, or unmapped land.

New World
    The name given by Europeans to North and South America after Columbus arrived in the region in 1492.

quasi
    Partial, or less than fully real.

ratify
    To give approval to a proposal such as a treaty.

Republican Party
    One of the two major political parties to emerge after the American Revolution; led by Thomas Jefferson, the Republicans supported greater individual states' rights and a weaker central, "federal" government. The Republican Party of 1800 is not the same as the Republican Party today.

secede
    To break away from a group, alliance, or nation.

treaty
    An agreement made between two nations.

Source Notes

Chapter 1. A Surprise Meeting

None.

Chapter 2. To the Frontier

1. Thomas Jefferson, "Letter to the Governor of Virginia (James Monroe)," *From Revolution to Reconstruction: A Hypertext on American History from the Colonial Period until Modern Times*. Department of Humanities Computing, University of Croningen, The Netherlands. 11 Nov. 2006 <http://odur.let.rug.nl/~usa/P/tj3/writings/brf/jefl142.htm>.

Chapter 3. Louisiana: The New World Colony

1. David Mills. *A Report on the Boundaries of the Province of Ontario*. Toronto: Hunter, Rose & Co., 1873. 5. Google Books. 15 Nov. 2006 <http://books.google.com/books?id=2C0qlS6XleYC&dq>.

Chapter 4. The Shifting Balance of Power

1. Alexander DeConde. *This Affair of Louisiana*. New York: Charles Scribner's Sons, 1976. 52.

2. Gilbert Din. "Spain's Immigration Policy in Louisiana and the American Penetration." *Washington D.C. American Historical Review* 102: 2. 601.

Chapter 5. Napoleon's Vision of Empire

1. Thomas Jefferson. "Letter to Samuel Du Pont de Nemours, April 1802." *The Napoleon Series*. 12 Nov. 2006 <http://www.napoleon-series.org/research/government/diplomatic/c_louisiana.html>.

Chapter 6. The American Dilemma: Jefferson Pursues Peace

1. John P. Foley, ed. "Letter to Dr. John Priestley, Jan. 1804." *The Jeffersonian Cyclopedia*. New York: Funk & Wagnalls, 1900. 525.

2. W. Wilson Lyon. "Louisiana in French Diplomacy." *Journal of Southern History* 2: 3. Aug. 1936. 161–162. JSTOR 15 Nov. 2006 <http://links.jstor.org/sici?sici=0022-4642(193608)2%3A3%3C408%3ALIFD1%3E2.0.CO%3B2-D>.

3. Peter Hicks. "Louisiana: to Have and to Have not…" *Napoleon.com*. 20 Nov. 2006 <http://www.napoleon.org/en/reading_room/articles/files/louisiana_hicks.asp>.

The Louisiana Purchase

Chapter 7. The Twists of Fate

1. Henry Steele Commager and Milton Cantor, eds. *Documents of American History*. Vol. 1. Englewood Cliffs, NJ: Prentice-Hall, 1899. 109.

2. Ibid.

3. Peter Hicks. "Louisiana: to Have and to Have not…" *Napoleon.com*. 20 Nov. 2006 <http://www.napoleon.org/en/reading_room/articles/files/louisiana_hicks.asp>.

4. Carl Ludwig Lokke. "The Leclerc Instructions." *The Journal of Negro History* 10: 1. Jan. 1925. 80–98. JSTOR. 23 Nov. 2006 <http://links.jstor.org/sici?sici=00222992(192501)10%3A1%3C80%3ATLI%3E2.0.CO%3B2-C>.

5. Albert Phelps. *Louisiana: A Record of Expansion*. New York: Houghton Mifflin and Company, 1905. 185. Google Books. 1 Dec. 2006 <http://books.google.com/books?id=gXLFqIGNX70C&dq=>.

6. Peter Hicks. "Louisiana: to Have and to Have not…" *Napoleon.com*. 20 Nov. 2006 <http://www.napoleon.org/en/reading_room/articles/files/louisiana_hicks.asp>.

Chapter 8. The Louisiana Purchase

1. Cardinal Goodwin. *The Trans-Mississippi West*. New York: D. Appleton and Company, 1922. 24–25. Google Books. 5 Dec. 2006 <http://books.google.com/books?id=cGcOAAAAIAAJ&pg=>.

2. Daniel Webster Wilder. *The Annals of Kansas*. Topeka, KS: G.W. Martin, 1875. 15. Google Books. 1 Dec. 2006 <http://books.google.com/books?vid=OCLC11515122&id=AOhPy_uiSSoC&pg=PP3&lpg=PP3&dq=>.

3. "The Letter that Bought an Empire." *American Heritage Magazine* Apr. 1955. *AmericanHeritage.com*. 15 Nov. 2006 <http://www.americanheritage.com/articles/magazine/ah/1955/3/1955_3_26.shtml>.

Source Notes Continued

Chapter 9. The Nation Doubles in Size Overnight

1. "The Louisiana Purchase Treaty, April 30, 1803." *The Avalon Project at Yale Law School.* 12 Nov. 2006 <http://www.yale.edu/lawweb/avalon/diplomacy/france/louis1.htm>.

2. George Morgan. *The Life of James Monroe.* New York: Small, Maynard, and Company, 1921. 252. Google Books. 18 Nov. 2006 <http://books.google.com/books?id=hhQOAAAAIAAJ&dq>.

3. Mary Kay Phelan. *The Story of the Louisiana Purchase,* New York: Thomas Y. Crowell, 1979. 102–103.

4. Tommy Rogers. "Threatened Secession by New England Over the Purchase of Louisiana and Other Grievances." Southeastern Events. 3 Dec. 2006 <http://www.southernevents.org/threatened_secession_by_new_engl.htm>.

Chapter 10. The New America

1. *Freedom: A History of US.* "Segment 9: An Empire for Liberty." PBS: Picture History and Educational Broadcasting. 2002. 12 June 2007 <http://www.pbs.org/wnet/historyofus/web02/segment9.html>.

Index

Adams, John, 36, 37, 41, 56
American Revolution, 14, 18
Appalachian Mountains, 8, 16–18
Atlantic Ocean, 38–39, 55

Barbé-Marbois, Francois de, 57, 60, 79–80, 83, 86
Bonaparte, Joseph, 11, 47, 55, 61, 76
Bonaparte, Lucien, 47, 76
Bonaparte, Napoleon
    as general, 43, 47–48, 56–57, 61–62, 69–72, 76–77
    Louisiana, 7, 9, 11–12, 49–52, 54–61, 65–68, 77–80, 83–84, 88

Canada, 8, 15, 29, 93
Cap Haitien, San Domingue, 69
Caribbean, 8, 11, 30–31, 43
Charles III, 30
Charles IV, 9, 43, 49, 71, 91
Claiborne, William, 92
Clark, William, 94
colonization, 43, 68
Congress, 10, 21, 41, 44, 52, 71–72, 86–88, 93

Declaration of Independence, 11, 56, 66
Decrès, Denis, 69
du Pont, Samuel, 52
du Pont de Nemours, Pierre, 66

England, 11, 15–17, 28–30, 35, 38, 40–41, 55–56, 66, 76–77, 86
Etruria, 49–50, 91

Federalists, 37–38, 86–88
Floridas, 12, 30, 44, 54, 58, 75–76, 79
Fort Crevecoeur, 26
France. *See also* Bonaparte, Napoleon; Louisiana Purchase
    relations with the U.S., 6–7, 10–12, 39–42, 57–61, 65–68, 74–76
    territories, 16, 25–29, 31, 49–52, 70–72
free trade, 9, 44, 59
French and Indian War, 29
French Republic, 42
French Revolution, 38–39, 46–47

Genêt, Edmund Charles Edouard, 39–40
guerilla war, 69–70
Gulf of Mexico, 17–18, 26, 29, 35, 59

Haiti. *See* San Domingue
Hamilton, Alexander, 18, 37

Irujo, Carlos, 91

Index Continued

Jay, John, 40
Jay Treaty, 41
Jefferson, Thomas, 18, 36, 37, 51, 56
  interest in western expansion, 22, 24–25, 93–94
  negotiating Louisiana Purchase, 7, 10–12, 41–42, 44, 54–57, 65–67, 71–72, 75–76, 84–86

La Salle, René Robert Cavelier Sieur de, 26–28
Laussat, Pierre Clement de, 91–92
Leclerc, Victor Emmanuel, 61–62, 69–70, 72
Lee, Charles, 32
Lewis, Meriwether, 94
Livingston, Robert, 6–7, 57–61, 66
Louis XIV, 26
Louis XV, 29–30
Louis XVI, 39
Louisiana Purchase. *See also* Jefferson, Thomas: negotiating Louisiana Purchase
  negotiation, 82–84
  price, 80
  public opinion, 90–92

Louisiana Territory, 27
  exploration of, 93–94
L'Ouverture, Toussaint, 62, 69
Lower Mississippi Territory, 36, 43, 52

Madison, James, 12, 18, 61, 65–66, 72, 80, 84
María Luísa, 49, 91
Mexico, 8, 30
Mississippi River, 7–9, 16, 26–28, 34–35, 57, 71, 75
Mississippi Territory, 44
Missouri River, 36, 94
Monroe, James, 7, 12, 22, 72, 74–77, 79–80, 83–84

National Intelligencer, 85
Native Americans, 25, 29, 44
New England, 87
New Orleans, Louisiana, 25, 30–35, 44, 57–59, 67, 71, 78, 83, 90–91
Northwest Ordinance, 20–21
Northwest Territory, 17, 24, 41

O'Reilly, Alexander, 31

Pacific Ocean, 22, 26, 28, 75, 93
Paris, France, 47, 57, 61, 74

The Louisiana Purchase

Pinckney's Treaty, 43
Pineda, Alonzo Álavarez, 26
Port-au-Prince, San Domingue, 69

Quasi War, 41, 52

Republicans, 37–38, 41, 86
Right of Deposit, 35, 57, 71, 75, 83
Rocky Mountains, 27, 94
Ross, James, 71

slave rebellion, 62, 68–70
Smith, Harrison, 85
Soto, Hernando de, 28
Spain
   relations with the U.S., 34–36, 42–44, 52, 83, 90–91
   territories, 8–9, 15, 29, 30–32, 49–51
San Domingue, 11, 16, 30, 61, 64, 69–70, 77

Talleyrand, Charles Maurice de, 6–7, 11–12, 59–60, 78–79
taxation, 35, 83
trade, 28, 35, 39, 41, 43–44, 57, 75, 93
Treaty of Amiens, 65, 76
Treaty of Paris, 14–15, 18

Treaty of San Ildefonso, 51–52, 54
Treaty of San Lorenzo, 43

Ulloa, Don Antonio de, 31
Union, 21, 84
Unzaga, Don Luis de, 32

Victor, Claude, 68–69, 77
Voyage of Discovery, 94

Washington, George, 18, 21, 29, 38, 40, 42
western expansion, 20, 37, 52, 57, 92, 94
Whiskey Rebellion, 21–22
White, Samuel, 87
Wilkinson, James, 38, 92

yellow fever, 70, 72, 77

About the Author

Jon Zurn is a journalist and author of works for both kids and adults. He is also editor of *Portrait of Achievement*, a magazine celebrating the work of young people across the United States. He studied history at the University of Wisconsin and currently lives in Minnesota.

Photo Credits

Architect of the Capitol, cover, 3; Stock Montage, 6, 13, 23, 33, 37, 98 (top), 99; North Wind Photo Archives, 14, 19, 20, 27, 34, 40, 46, 50, 53, 58, 60, 68, 73, 82, 96, 97; Corbis, 24; Bettmann/Corbis, 45, 54, 89; AP Images, 63, 95, 98 (bottom); Rischgitz/Getty Images, 64; General Records of the U.S. Government, National Archives/AP Images, 74; MPI/Getty Images, 81; Hulton Archive/Getty Images, 90